Volodymyr Zelenskyy

Ukrainian President and Unlikely Hero

Don Nardo

ReferencePoint Press®

San Diego, CA

© 2023 ReferencePoint Press, Inc.
Printed in the United States

For more information, contact:
ReferencePoint Press, Inc.
PO Box 27779
San Diego, CA 92198
www.ReferencePointPress.com

LIBRARY OF CONGRESS CATALOGING-IN-PUBLICATION DATA

Names: Nardo, Don, 1947- author.
Title: Volodymyr Zelenskyy : Ukrainian President and unlikely hero / Don
    Nardo.
Description: San Diego : ReferencePoint Press, 2022. | Includes
    bibliographical references and index.
Identifiers: LCCN 2022029380 (print) | LCCN 2022029381 (ebook) | ISBN
    9781678204907 (library binding) | ISBN 9781678204914 (ebook)
Subjects: LCSH: Zelenskyy, Volodymyr, 1978- |
    Presidents--Ukraine--Biography. | Ukraine--Politics and government--21st
    century. | Ukraine--Foreign relations--Russia (Federation) | Russia
    (Federation)--Foreign relations--Ukraine. | Leadership--Western countries.
Classification: LCC DK508.851.Z45 N37 2023 (print) | LCC DK508.851.Z45
    (ebook) | DDC 947.7086092 [B]--dc23/eng/20220630
LC record available at https://lccn.loc.gov/2022029380
LC ebook record available at https://lccn.loc.gov/2022029381

Contents

Commitment, Courage, and an Indomitable Spirit

On February 24, 2022, news bulletins interrupted radio and television programs around the world to report that Russian missiles had begun to rain down on various targets in the nation of Ukraine. Situated directly west of Poland, in eastern Europe, Ukraine is a former Soviet territory. In 1991, when the Soviet Union collapsed, Ukraine became an independent nation. That had never sat well with Russian president Vladimir Putin. In his view, Ukraine had always been and should always be part of Russia. In February 2022, therefore, he launched an invasion designed to bring the Ukrainians back into the Russian fold.

Putin's Propaganda Blitz

In response to the incursion, Ukraine's president, Volodymyr Zelenskyy (sometimes also spelled Zelensky), hastily marshaled his nation's military forces. A former actor and comedian, Zelenskyy had been elected president in 2019. It was his first foray into national politics. During his first years in office, critics questioned whether he was up to the task of running a country. With the invasion underway, many worried that he lacked the experience and fortitude to deal with a major political and military strongman like Putin.

4

Indeed, as the attack began, Putin, formerly a member of the Soviet Union's secret security and spy organization—the KGB—immediately launched a major propaganda blitz. Its main goal was to paint Zelenskyy as incompetent and cowardly. Hoping to create confusion and dampen the spirit of the Ukrainian people, Putin's propaganda operatives tried to promote the idea that Zelenskyy had fled the capital, Kyiv, leaving the Ukrainian people in the lurch.

This falsehood-ridden rant by Putin and his propaganda network failed miserably, however. Despite his lack of experience in politics and military matters, Zelenskyy swiftly demonstrated a level of competency and courage that exposed the Russian narrative as a tattered tissue of lies. Zelenskyy immediately countered the invaders' untruths about him by having his own operatives film him walking through Kyiv's main streets. This footage showed the Ukrainian president calmly strolling along, clearly very much in charge and seemingly unfazed by the ongoing Russian onslaught.

A Proverbial Backbone of Steel

Zelenskyy also showed that he possesses a mastery of social media, a talent that Putin notoriously lacks. In a series of well-timed and well-worded tweets, the Ukrainian leader shrewdly

The damage in Ukraine as a result of Russia's 2022 invasion has been devastating. Ukraine's president, Volodymyr Zelenskyy, has quickly shown that he is up to the task of leading his country against Russia's attack.

condemned the invaders. One of Zelenskyy's first international tweets stated, "Russia treacherously attacked our [nation this] morning, as Nazi Germany did in [World War II]. As of today, our countries are on different sides of world history. Russia has embarked on a path of evil, but Ukraine is defending itself and won't give up its freedom no matter what Moscow thinks."[1]

Zelenskyy soon confirmed that these words were not mere temporary bravado but rather a sign that he had a proverbial backbone of steel. In the first few days of the conflict, bands of Russian military operatives snuck into Kyiv bent on assassinating him and his family. Putin apparently hoped that taking Zelenskyy out would spread fear and demoralize the Ukrainian people. It proved to be another of Putin's growing list of failures. Hearing that he had been targeted for death, Zelenskyy shrugged and told his assistants that he had expected such a move by Putin. The Ukrainian leader's disciplined reaction was first to alert his bodyguards to the threat and second to go on running the country.

Putin was not the only world leader who was surprised by Zelenskyy's well-ordered, unflinching attitude during the early moments of the crisis. Expecting the Russian army to take Kyiv in fairly short order, US and British officials had moved swiftly to help preserve Ukraine's democratic government. Meeting with Zelenskyy, they offered to evacuate him and his family and staff to a neighboring country, where he could set up a government in exile. That way, when Putin installed a Russian-friendly puppet regime in Kyiv, the *real* Ukrainian government could go on functioning.

However, Zelenskyy politely but firmly turned down the offer. In so doing he uttered ten words that revealed his commitment to the job of leading his country, his courage, and an indomitable spirit. "The fight is here," Zelenskyy told the US and British officials. "I need ammunition, not a ride."[2]

6

Chapter One

From Hometown Boy to Popular Comedian

In 2020 the Jewish president of Ukraine, Volodymyr Zelenskyy, traveled to Israel and met with Israeli prime minister Benjamin Netanyahu. The main goal of the trip was to mark the seventy-fifth anniversary of the liberation of the World War II Nazi death camp Auschwitz, in Poland. Zelenskyy noted that the Nazis killed more than 1 million Ukrainian Jews during the war.

Then the Ukrainian leader got more personal by telling his host the wartime tale of, in Zelenskyy's words, "a family of four brothers." All members of the Zelenskyy family, they had grown up in the same Ukrainian village in the early 1900s and had joined the Soviet army to fight the Nazis. Three of the four brothers, Zelenskyy recalled, along with all the members of their families, "were shot by German occupiers who invaded Ukraine. The fourth brother [Semyon Zelenskyy] survived. [Later], two years after the war, he had a son, and in 31 years, he had a grandson. In 40 more years, that grandson became president [of Ukraine], and he is standing before you today, Mr. Prime Minister."[3]

> "Two years after [World War II, my grandfather] had a son, and in 31 years, he had a grandson. In 40 more years, that grandson became president [of Ukraine], and he is standing before you today."[3]
>
> —Volodymyr Zelenskyy

In 2020 Zelenskyy met with Israeli prime minister Benjamin Netanyahu and shared that his family had joined the Soviet fight against the Nazis during World War II. Zelenskyy is pictured here (on the right) at a 2019 meeting with Netanyahu.

Youth and Education

The story told to Netanyahu about the four brothers in World War II was only a sketchy summary of the larger, more detailed saga of the Zelenskyy family. In the longer version, after the war ended Semyon Zelenskyy got married and in 1947 had a son named Oleksandr. The latter then met a well-educated young woman named Rymma, and the two fell in love and married. They settled in the small city of Kryvyy Rih, in central Ukraine.

It was there, on January 25, 1978, that Rymma gave birth to the couple's only child, Volodymyr. Both parents were employed full time. Oleksandr was a professor of computer science at the local college—Kryvyy Rih State University—and Rymma worked as an engineer. In part because they were both highly educated, they imparted to their son the importance of learning and encouraged him in his studies, including languages. Although he initially grew up speaking Russian, young Volodymyr mastered both Ukrainian and English in his early to mid-teens.

Although the young man considered Kryvyy Rih his hometown, he did experience a brief break from its familiar surroundings. In the mid-1980s Oleksandr decided to do firsthand scientific research in the distant Mongolian town of Erdenet, situated thousands of miles to the east. The family endured four years of frigid winter temperatures before moving back to Ukraine.

While in high school in Kryvyy Rih, Volodymyr met his future wife, Olena Kiyashko. They dated on and off, and after graduating in 1995, both went on to attend the local Kryvyy Rih Economic Institute. Olena majored in architecture but spent most of her spare time writing screenplays and working with a campus organization that promoted women's rights.

Meanwhile, Volodymyr was studying law. However, he too was drawn into other activities in his spare time, principally aspects of the theater and performing. He had long been fascinated by acting, especially playing comic roles and telling jokes. In 1995, while still a freshman at the institute, he formed a *Saturday Night Live*–style group of comedic performers called Kvartal 95, which translates into English as either "Quarter 95" or "Neighborhood 95." For two years the group improvised and rehearsed comic sketches until Volodymyr felt they were ready to go public. In 1997 he entered the group into the popular Ukrainian TV competition called *KVN*, which stood for "Club of the Funny and Inventive People." The show, which was broadcast in Ukraine and several neighboring countries, had an audience in the millions. Kvartal 95 was an instant hit and by public demand became a regular attraction on the program until 2003.

Success in Stand-Up and Founding a Family

Zelenskyy graduated from the institute in 2000 with a law degree. If he had been so inclined, he could have begun a career as an attorney. But by that time he was hooked on the performing arts. His comedy troupe performed fairly regularly, not only on television but also in local stage shows around the country.

Also, thanks to the exposure he had received on *KVN*, talent agents contacted him fairly regularly. This enabled him to do small roles in Ukrainian films, as well as get gigs as a stand-up comic. He performed his stand-up routine far and wide, including in Ukrainian, Russian, and even Israeli cities. (Over the preceding decades many Ukrainian Jews, including Zelenskyy's own great-aunt, had immigrated to Israel, so Ukrainian Jewish performers had a ready and receptive audience there.) In 2006 Zelenskyy told an Israeli newspaper reporter that he had done the stand-up routine in "Tel Aviv, in Beersheba, in Haifa, and in Jerusalem. In so many cities. So I know Israel. . . . I know people there."[4] Also in 2006, he performed on and won the popular *Strictly Come Dancing* television competition, the Ukrainian equivalent of America's *Dancing with the Stars*.

During these same eventful years, Zelenskyy also continued to date his school sweetheart, Olena. In 2003 they decided to make it official and got married. The following year they had a daughter, whom they named Oleksandra, after Zelenskyy's father. And several years later, in 2013, came a son. His parents chose for him the name Kyrylo, meaning "the Lord," which had long been a popular name among Ukrainian Jews.

Like a Pro on the Dance Floor

Popular British journalist Meghna Amin here provides a review of Zelenskyy's multiple 2006 appearances on *Strictly Come Dancing*, the Ukrainian version of *Dancing with the Stars*. After Russia invaded Ukraine in early 2022, millions of people around the world watched YouTube videos of Zelenskyy dancing and were suitably amazed at his skill and professional demeanor. As Amin puts it:

As Ukrainian President Volodymyr Zelensky has proven himself to be one of the most courageous leaders in living memory, his epic triumph in the country's [version of] *Dancing With The Stars* is blowing people around the world away. . . . In a video that was shared on Twitter . . . and swiftly spread across social media, President Zelensky is seen waltzing, performing the pase doble, and quickstep all across the ballroom, looking very much like a pro. He's seen with his dance partner Olena Shoptenko showing off his moves to classic songs like Elvis Presley's Blue Suede Shoes and the Pink Panther theme song. With many already recognizing him as a hero, the compilation video has now shown a completely different, yet just as popular, side of him, displaying how natural he is on a dancefloor and in front of the cameras.

Meghna Amin, "Ukrainian President Volodymyr Zelensky Actually Won *Dancing with the Stars* and Gave the Pros a Good Run for Their Money," *Metro* (London), 2022. https://metro.co.uk.

In 2003 Zelenskyy married his school sweetheart, Olena Kiyashko, pictured here with him in 2019.

National Television and Feature Films

For Zelenskyy, 2003 turned out to be productive in ways other than starting a family. Also that year he cofounded Studio Kvartal 95, a film company that was destined to become one of his country's best-known and most successful entertainment studios. Zelenskyy served as the company's artistic director during the decade that followed. In October 2012 he and Studio Kvartal 95 signed a joint production agreement with 1+1, Ukraine's largest television network. It was owned by one of the country's richest individuals, Ihor Kolomoisky, who was eager to cash in on Zelenskyy's obvious talent and growing popularity.

In the next three years, while working on TV programs, Zelenskyy and his company coproduced some feature films for movie theaters. The first one, launched in late 2012, was a joint production with the Russian film company Leopolis. It was a historical farce titled *Rzhevskiy Versus Napoleon*. The film, in which Zelenskyy delivers a comic portrayal of the French dictator and military general Napoléon Bonaparte, takes place in 1812. Napoléon's forces have invaded Russia and are about to attack the major Russian city of St. Petersburg. A group of Russian patriots decide to try to distract the French leader through a desperate and daring romantic escapade. In the scheme, a Russian army officer named Rzhevskiy dresses up as a woman and attempts to woo the enormously arrogant Napoléon, with predictably silly but funny results.

The movie was not financially successful. It cost $8.5 million to make but took in only $7.8 million at the box office in its first run. Still, the project helped cement Zelenskyy's reputation as a comic actor of high standing. Two more feature films soon followed, the romantic comedies *8 First Dates* (2013) and *8 New Dates* (2015).

An Unlikely Series of Events

The energetic Zelenskyy had no sooner wrapped up filming of *8 New Dates* than he began to work on the project that would change his life and the history of his country in ways more profound than anyone then alive could imagine. Namely, the 1+1 studio started production on the innovative television series *Servant of the People*. Conceived and produced by Zelenskyy himself, the plot revolves around Vasily Petrovych Goloborodko, a highschool history teacher in his thirties.

Still living with his parents, Goloborodko, played by Zelenskyy, is mild-mannered and views politics in a largely idealistic manner. Then one day he is suddenly drawn into an unlikely series of events that popular NPR film critic Eric Deggans here summarizes:

> Packing up his things after a class, the history teacher spouts off to a friend, burning with frustration over the government's corruption, the public's apathy, and how a secretive group of oligarchs—always depicted in dark rooms scheming over luxurious food and drink, run everything from the shadows. One of his students secretly films the expletive-laden tirade and posts it online. When it catches

the country's attention, his pupils create a crowd-funding platform which raises enough money for a campaign. In a flash, he's elected to the presidency.[5]

Having been thrust into the presidency, Goloborodko must now try to live up to the ideals and standards he set in the angry rant his student posted online. "You're servants of the people," the former teacher tells the Ukrainian politicians when he first meets with them. "In actuality, the Greek word 'democracy' translates as 'rule *of* the people,' not 'rule *over* the people.' Where does it say that servants should live better than their masters?"[6]

This principled, ethical attitude does not go down well with many of the country's politicians, who are used to selfishly using their powerful positions to advance and enrich themselves. And Goloborodko is dismayed when he witnesses some of his own friends and relatives trying to cash in on the fact that they are connected to the new president. He sticks to his high standards, however, as exemplified by one of his public speeches. After noticing that some of his former students are in the audience, he discards the empty words written by his aides and speaks from his heart, saying, "This is some story. A history teacher makes it

Film-Directing Skills, Too!

In 2018 many people in Ukraine, as well as in nations around the world, were delighted to discover that in addition to his skills as an actor, comedian, and dancer, Volodymyr Zelenskyy could also direct films. That year his production company released the romantic comedy *Me. You. He. She.* which he codirected (with American director David Dodson) and starred in. The plot revolves around Maxim and his wife, Yana, who have been married for ten years. Unfortunately for them, the passion has gone out of the relationship, and they stay together more out of duty and mutual respect than love. Each becomes attracted to someone else, so they file for divorce. According to Ukrainian law, however, they have a month's waiting period before the decree becomes final, and in that interval they decide to act out various love-related fantasies they dared not do before, with heartwarming results. The film's financial success can be seen in its raw figures. It cost $1.3 million to make and in the initial, brief box office period alone grossed $2.7 million.

into history. I do know one thing: One should act in a way that doesn't evoke shame when looking into children's eyes. . . . This is what I promise you, the people of Ukraine."[7]

A Wealthy Person Indeed

To Zelenskyy's delight, *Servant of the People* turned out to be an instant and huge hit. An estimated 20 million Ukrainian households tuned in on their TV sets to watch the show's first season. And as many as 95 million people in Ukraine and surrounding countries saw those episodes on YouTube, which Zelenskyy contracted with to carry the program. *Servant* was so popular, in fact, that in late 2016 Studio Kvartal 95 produced a feature film based on it—*Servant of the People 2*. Moreover, excerpts from the movie were used in the TV version's second and third seasons, which aired during 2017 to 2019.

Zelenskyy's acting, producing, and sharing in the profits from 1+1 and Studio Kvartal 95 made him very wealthy. He is shown here in 2018, during Studio Kvartal 95's concert program.

Zelenskyy saw the wisdom of taking advantage of the ongoing lucrative situation by quickly investing in other TV and film projects. The most notable of these was Studio Kvartal 95's 2018 romantic comedy movie titled *Me. You. He. She*. Only a few months after its release, it proved to be the most profitable feature film ever made in Ukraine.

At that point, Zelenskyy was easily one of Ukraine's most famous public figures. He was also one of the country's richest citizens. The combination of his comedy work, acting, producing, and sharing in the profits garnered by both 1+1 and Studio Kvartal 95 had made him a very wealthy person. He was able to support at least three family homes inside Ukraine, along with a large, luxurious villa in northern Italy (which was reportedly valued at $4.8 million in 2022).

The value of Zelenskyy's business interests was measurable in round numbers. Less certain was the potential worth of the unique and still widely popular idea behind *Servant of the People*. Family members, friends, and coworkers periodically told him that, if he really wanted to, he could almost certainly use the publicity and goodwill the show had created to actually run for president. The next presidential election was slated for 2019. If he ran and managed to win, they pointed out, he could introduce the same sort of political reforms that his character, Goloborodko, had in the fictional story.

No one knows for sure exactly when Zelenskyy decided that his life could credibly imitate his art. However, in late 2018 he officially registered a new political party with the government. When asked what name the party would bear, he replied without hesitation: Servant of the People.

Chapter Two

A Very Modern-Style Politician and Leader

"Glory to Ukraine!,"[8] Volodymyr Zelenskyy shouted. He delivered those words in a clear, resonant voice, coupled with a sincere air of pride in his country. And everyone who heard him speak them, including those who disagreed with his political and social views, could sense their genuineness. Clearly, he did not utter those words for the sake of political expediency or to curry favor with his fans. Rather, there could be no doubt that they came directly from his heart.

What made the speech containing those words particularly special was that it was not a piece of scripted dialogue from one of Zelenskyy's television, film, or YouTube performances. Instead, he delivered the address from an elegant, hand-carved wooden lectern in the Verkhovna Rada, the Ukrainian parliament, in downtown Kyiv. The country's 450 legislators, called deputies, along with various invited guests, had convened there on May 20, 2019, to hear the country's new president—a former actor and comedian—give his inaugural speech. "Dear Nation!," Zelenskyy told the audience in the hall. "All my life I tried to do all I could so that Ukrainians laughed. That was my mission. Now I will do all I can so that Ukrainians at least do not cry any more."[9]

The Decision to Run for Office

Some of the people who heard Zelenskyy speak that day were amazed that a person who had made his name strictly as an entertainer had managed to win the presidency—and in a virtual landslide. Yet those Ukrainians who knew, admired, and believed in him were not at all surprised by his win. They knew, as he did, that he had attained the highest office in the land the same way he had achieved success in other areas. He had done it through a combination of genuine talent and hard work.

At first, back in 2018 when some of Zelenskyy's friends and aides suggested he might run for the presidency, he had been unsure about seriously following that path. On the one hand, he was quite happy being a successful actor, producer, director, and comedian. On the other, he realized that, at least temporarily, he would need to put his chosen field and pursuits aside and unselfishly devote himself to serving his country and fellow citizens.

The more Zelenskyy thought about it, the more he reasoned that public service would be a good way of paying back the public for making him an adored and wealthy individual. There was another issue to consider, nonetheless. Namely, he wondered whether he could be a good president. Eventually, he came to believe that he could and *would*. In part, what convinced him was a series of frank conversations with relatives and friends. They repeatedly pointed out that his television show *Servant of the People* was the key. The character he portrayed on that program, Goloborodko, they said, was an honest, caring, dedicated, hardworking, natural-born leader. Furthermore, they added, Zelenskyy himself was all those things, too. After all, in creating the character and show, he tried to make Goloborodko in many ways a reflection of himself. Finally, his closer confidants told him, many Ukrainians already assumed that there were real similarities between Goloborodko and Zelenskyy. So he had a sort of built-in public support base already, something any politician would envy.

> "All my life I tried to do all I could so that Ukrainians laughed."[9]
>
> —Volodymyr Zelenskyy in his inaugural address

Having considered all these facts and arguments, Zelenskyy had a final, long heart-to-heart talk with his wife, Olena, to make sure it would be all right with her if he campaigned for the presidency. She told him she had her reservations, since their lives would inevitably change in various ways, including becoming more hectic. But she also wanted him to be happy, she said, and if running would achieve that, she would not stand in the way. Moreover, she made the point that in her view the country would be lucky to have someone as talented and honest as he was for its leader.

What Did Ukrainians Worry About Most?

The decision to run having been made, Zelenskyy went ahead and registered his political party, Servant of the People. That was only a tiny first step, he realized. Much planning and hard work would follow. One initial question was which issues and policies to concentrate on in his campaign. At first, he was somewhat unsure of some of them, partly because he had never been a politician before. Therefore, at the outset he had no well-developed platform, or set of party or governmental goals. Instead, at first, political observers Tanya Tanyarattinan and Josh Wilson point out, his team crowdsourced ideas from his followers on social media. This led to one of the most common criticisms against Zelensky during his campaign: that he had no political vision of his own. However, his supporters spun this positively, saying that he was showing that he wanted to know how the public wanted to be governed before telling the public how it should be governed. In fact, one of the most central promises to his political platform, released in late January, 2019, is to make strong use of public referendums, particularly through the Internet, to determine the government's agenda and direction.[10]

The Territorial Issue

One problem that troubled many Ukrainians was the considerable loss of territory in recent years to Russia. Zelenskyy had some specific ideas about how to address that issue, which had surfaced in 2014. That year Russia, under President Vladimir Putin, had seized control of Crimea, the southernmost sector of Ukraine, situated on the Black Sea's northern shores. Crimea had for generations been part of Ukraine. Despite having no legal authority to intervene in Ukrainian affairs, Putin had announced that Crimea was now an independent republic. Its leaders had requested to make Crimea part of Russia, he claimed, offering no acceptable evidence.

"His team crowdsourced ideas from his followers on social media. This led to one of the most common criticisms against Zelensky during his campaign: that he had no political vision of his own."[10]

—Tanya Tanyarattinan and Josh Wilson, political observers

Under Ukraine's president at the time, Petro Poroshenko, the Ukrainians had loudly protested this naked land grab. Moreover, the vast majority of countries belonging to the United Nations, including the United States and other Western nations, condemned Russia's seizure of Crimea. But Putin had simply ignored these objections, and Poroshenko had not taken the land back.

Russian soldiers march in the Crimean city of Perevalne in 2014, after Russia seized control of Crimea from Ukraine, despite protests from Ukraine and many other countries.

That same year the Russians had also targeted the Donbas, Ukraine's easternmost region. Russian operatives had stirred up trouble by supporting and arming groups of local people who had long felt that Ukraine would be better off under Russian control. These self-described separatists took over several government buildings in the Donbas's subregions of Donetsk and Luhansk and began openly fighting with Ukrainians who did not share their views. The unrest continued there into early 2019.

Confronting the Country's Leading Crisis

Zelenskyy and his campaign staff strongly emphasized these simmering separatist issues and repeatedly called the Russian presence in the Donbas the country's leading crisis. In numerous public interviews and speeches, he addressed that crisis, asserting that the best way to end the hostilities in the eastern separatist regions was to employ a twofold approach. First, he said, if elected president he would work to create a cease-fire in the disputed areas. He repeated this vow in his inaugural address.

I have been often asked what price are you ready to pay for the ceasefire? It's a strange question. What price are you ready to pay for the lives of your loved ones? I can assure you that I'm ready to pay any price to stop the deaths of our heroes. I'm definitely not afraid to make difficult decisions, and I'm ready to lose my fame, my ratings, and if need be—without any hesitation, my position to bring peace, as long as we do not give up our territories.[11]

Second, Zelenskyy said repeatedly during the campaign—and after his election—that he would intensify diplomatic efforts to reach an acceptable solution to the crisis in the Donbas. He emphasized that his opponent in the race, Poroshenko, who was still serving as president, had failed to solve the separatist-related problems. In spite of claiming that he would fix the problem, a great deal of Ukrainian land was now controlled by Russian soldiers. "We will not give up," Zelenskyy said in one of his most celebrated speeches. He and the members of his government would do whatever was necessary to restore the usurped territories. "We will continue fighting for our land, whatever the cost,"[12] he promised.

First Lady Olena Zelenska

As she has revealed in multiple interviews since 2020, Ukraine's First Lady, Olena Zelenska, was initially not comfortable with the notion of her husband running for the presidency. She has described herself as a private person and has said that the thought of making frequent public appearances as First Lady initially made her nervous. "I am a non-public person," she explained in a 2022 interview. Nevertheless, she has adjusted to the reality of her husband's role as president, but she has also set boundaries for herself and her family.

I prefer staying backstage. My husband is always on the forefront, while I feel more comfortable in the shade. I am not the life of the party, I do not like to tell jokes. It's not in my character. But I found reasons for myself in favor of publicity. One of them is the opportunity to attract people's attention to important social issues. At the same time, this does not concern the publicity of my children: I have not posted their photos on social networks before, and now I will not either.

Quoted in Emily Burack, "Who Is Ukrainian First Lady Olena Zelenska?," *Town & Country*, May 9, 2022. www.townandcountrymag.com.

Two other issues that Zelenskyy emphasized during the campaign were Ukraine's economic stability and national security. On the topic of the economy, he repeatedly told his countrymen what he would later echo no less strongly in his inaugural address, namely, "We must not just talk about [achieving comfortable Western] standards [here in Ukraine]. We must create those standards."[13]

The nation's economic health and its security would both be significantly enhanced, Zelenskyy said, if Ukraine sought closer ties with European and other Western countries. The old, traditional ties with Russia had gotten Ukraine nothing of any consequence, he insisted, except for bully tactics by thugs like Putin. In contrast, Zelenskyy emphasized often during the campaign, Europe and its allies had sincere interests in investing large amounts of money in Ukrainian industries, markets, and products.

He also pointed out that some of the Western countries had considered bringing Ukraine into the large-scale security alliance, the North Atlantic Treaty Organization (NATO). This would be

During his presidential campaign, Zelenskyy stressed the importance of seeking closer ties with European and other Western countries. He argued that Ukraine's ties with Russia had led to bullying by Russian president Vladimir Putin, pictured here in 2019.

helpful for the Ukrainians, he explained, because an attack on any single NATO nation is considered an attack on all of them, and that would make Russia and any other would-be aggressors think twice about attacking Ukraine. "We have chosen a path to Europe," Zelenskyy said, "but Europe is not somewhere out there. Europe is here [indicating his head]. And after it appears here, it will be everywhere, all over Ukraine."[14]

Zelenskyy's pro-Western leanings came up often during his presidential campaign—a fact not lost on Putin. The Russian president had harbored long-simmering frustration over what he perceived as his nation's lost glory and power in world affairs. Typical of Putin's reactions was his accusation that Zelenskyy and other Ukrainian authorities were "duping" and "making fools of millions of people."[15]

Every Ukrainian Now President?

By contrast, Zelenskyy used a far more moderate tone in almost all his campaign speeches. Although he was often critical of his opponent, Poroshenko, he was not rude and mostly either defended his own values or clarified his positions on various issues. When Poroshenko accused him of being a typical self-promoting politician and a puppet of superrich businesspeople, Zelenskyy countered by saying, in a matter-of-fact tone, "I'm not a politician. I'm an ordinary person who came to break this [ineffective] system [of yours]."[16]

> "I'm not a politician. I'm an ordinary person who came to break this [ineffective] system [of yours]."[16]
>
> —Volodymyr Zelenskyy

Zelenskyy's campaign was not only moderate in tone but also sought to avoid taking strong stands one way or another on controversial issues. For example, ever since they had become independent from the Russians three decades before, the Ukrainians had viewed language as a touchy subject. Many Ukrainians still spoke mainly Russian, while many others chose to speak only Ukrainian in order to make themselves appear more patriotic. Zelenskyy tried to take a middle-ground approach on

23

An Appeal to Ukrainians Everywhere

One of the major themes of Zelenskyy's inaugural address in April 2019 was that all Ukrainians were in a sense taking the oath of the presidency with him because all Ukrainians were in the same situation together and very much responsible for one another. To illustrate that idea, he said in part:

This is our common dream. But we also share a common pain. Each of us has died in the Donbas. Every day we lose each one of us. And each of us is a refugee, the one who has lost his own home and the one who has opened the door of his home, sharing the pain. . . . But we will overcome all of this! Because each of us is a Ukrainian. We are all Ukrainians. There are no bigger or lesser, or correct, or incorrect Ukrainians. . . . After all, only then we are strong. Today I appeal to all Ukrainians in the world. There are 65 million of us [including] those born on the Ukrainian soil, [plus] Ukrainians in Europe and Asia, in North and South America, Australia and Africa. I appeal to all Ukrainians on the planet! We really need you.

Quoted in *Ukrainian Weekly* (Jersey City, NJ), "Volodymyr Zelenskyy's Inaugural Address," May 24, 2019. www.ukrweekly.com.

the matter. Ukrainian should certainly be promoted as a language, he stated, but at the same time, Russian should not be prohibited or discouraged. Both were integral to the Ukrainian people, who should all be respectful of one another's cultural choices.

This conciliatory approach was among the factors that contributed to Zelenskyy's victory in the election in April 2019. In a massive landslide, he won a whopping 73 percent of the vote. Following that dramatic event, many members of the media immediately began wondering aloud what kind of president Zelenskyy would now become. His campaign, they admitted, had portrayed him as a real version of the humble, honest man of the people he had played on *Servant of the People*. But how would he actually govern?

In an attempt to answer that question, during his first few months in office, some reporters and political writers compared the text of the character Goloborodko's inauguration speech on the show to real public speeches given by the newly elected Zelenskyy. Goloborodko did not want to tell the people he would do something and later not be able to follow through. So, the fictional character stated, "I won't make any promises." Instead, he would do his best to "try to figure it out. But I do know one thing. One should act in a way that doesn't evoke shame when looking into children's eyes. Nor their parents'. Nor your (own) eyes, of course. This is what I promise you, the people of Ukraine."[17]

In comparison, Zelenskyy said in his own inaugural address that in a sense he was not the only person who had just taken an oath to protect and defend the country. "Each of us has just put his hand on the Constitution and swore allegiance to Ukraine," he suggested. In a statement that seemed to foreshadow a fresh, positive new era of Ukrainian government and politics, he added:

Now, imagine the headlines: "The President Does Not Pay Taxes," "The Intoxicated President Ran the Red Light" or "The President Is Quietly Stealing Because Everyone Does." Would you agree that it's shameful? This is what I mean when I say that each of us is the president. From now on, each of us is responsible for the country that we leave to our children. Each of us, in his place, can do every-thing for the prosperity of Ukraine.[18]

Chapter Three

First Three Years as President

In mid-May 2021, a man standing just five feet seven inches—called average-looking by some and ruggedly handsome by others—stood in front of a Ukrainian national flag in a government building in Kyiv. There was an air of confidence about him as he spoke to the gathered reporters. "We are building a country without oligarchs," President Volodymyr Zelenskyy announced. "We are killing the idea of an oligarch system in our country."[19]

The oligarchic system was, and in some cases still is, widely common in the former Soviet lands, including Ukraine. A relatively few superrich businesspeople–who hold a great deal of influence over the nation's economic and political life, the Ukrainian oligarchs are primarily the owners of valuable monopolies. Indeed, a journalist for Britain's BBC news organization comments, "The oligarchs' well-funded tentacles now reach deep into Ukrainian society. Many have their own political parties, and supportive television stations. Some also have judges and senior civil servants ready to do their bidding if the need arises."[20]

During the presidential campaign, Zelenskyy vowed that he would try to reduce the influence of the oligarchs in Ukraine. Once in office, he made good on that pledge by requesting the drafting of a bill that would place restrictions on those powerful individuals. In describing the bill, Zelenskyy noted, "There will be no influence on mass media, no influence on politics, no influence on officials. But if there *is* influence, then these people will get a ticket called 'oligarch.' They will be included in a special register, and then this big business may lose a great share of its assets."[21]

That Zelenskyy had become so anti-oligarch after gaining the presidency surprised some Ukrainians. During the presidential campaign he had been roundly criticized for his ties to the oligarch Ihor Kolomoisky, owner of the 1+1 television network, which had produced Zelenskyy's shows. Zelenskyy had answered such accusations by saying that as an actor he had lacked the power to reform the corrupted system, whereas as president he now had such authority.

Many Ukrainians applauded these efforts by Zelenskyy to make the country more democratic and less beholden to wealthy special interests. Some others were less impressed, however, and assumed that the president's efforts against the oligarchs were merely a public relations, or PR, stunt. In the words of one former

Zelenskyy—speaking on the right—and Petro Poroshenko (Ukraine's president from 2014–2019) engage in a debate prior to Ukraine's 2019 presidential election. During his campaign, Zelenskyy vowed to reduce the influence of the country's oligarchs.

government official, Oleksandr Danylyuk, "This is just PR. Going against oligarchs looks good for him. People like a president who is decisive and going after oligarchs and bandits."[22]

Enhancing the Powers of Citizens

Zelenskyy ultimately proved Danylyuk wrong. After taking office the new president followed through on his promises. The deputies of the Verkhovna Rada did not pass every law and policy change he proposed. But they did approve a fair number of them, including the one dealing with Ukraine's oligarchs. Not only did the new law create a registry—or public list and official record—of the oligarchs, it also prohibited oligarchs from financing political campaigns, which reduced their ability to control members of the legislature. In turn, by default, the new law placed more power in the hands of the ordinary citizens who elect those legislators.

Similarly, Zelenskyy managed to push through another new law that enhanced the powers of the country's citizenry. It provided Ukrainians with the right to hold periodic referenda, or national votes on specific issues. The preamble of the law's actual wording states, "The All-Ukrainian referendum is a form of direct

More Recognition of Jewish Contributions

The legislation reducing the powers of the oligarchs, which Zelenskyy proposed and pushed through Ukraine's parliament, was widely controversial. Much less provocative and more universally accepted by Ukrainians in general was his attempt to have the country better recognize its Jewish heritage and citizenry.

This was driven in part by his sense of fair play and, not surprisingly, his own Jewish family background. Among other things, the new bill called for renaming streets and monuments around Ukraine, replacing old Soviet names with those of Ukrainian heroes, both Jewish and non-Jewish. When Zelenskyy ran for the presidency, some Jewish Ukrainians, though appreciative of this idea, worried that it might backfire. Perhaps, they said, it might incite some of the anti-Semitic elements in the country to violence. This fear ultimately proved groundless, however. Zelenskyy's legislation failed to cause any sort of uproar or violent responses. Most Ukrainians had no objection to the new law, which, in addition to renaming streets, included the construction of a new memorial at Babi Yar, a deep ravine located on Kyiv's outskirts. There, during World War II, the Nazis murdered more than one hundred thousand Ukrainian Jews and other people whom Adolf Hitler deemed inferior.

democracy in Ukraine, a way of exercising power directly by the Ukrainian people through approving by the citizens of Ukraine of decisions by voting."[23]

Zelenskyy argued that the people should have a say in the nation's laws. For instance, they should be able to alter provisions in existing laws when changes are warranted or eliminate laws considered to be unjust. (*Not* subject to a national referendum would be changing laws that guard fundamental citizens' rights and freedoms.) "Now," Zelenskyy stated at the ceremony in which he signed the new law into effect, "Ukrainians will in real practice be involved in making decisions that are important for the country, and the government will have to listen to the will of the people."[24]

Zelenskyy's Positions on Social Issues

That theme—the will of the people—also informed Zelenskyy's public positions on a number of social issues. Opinion polls had shown that most Ukrainians supported moderately progressive social policies. A majority of Ukrainians favored legal abortion, for instance. Thus, Zelenskyy saw no reason to seek restrictions on abortion.

Likewise, Ukrainians were largely accepting of gambling and prostitution. For this reason, he concluded, both practices should be legal—within limits. He has cited the example of legal gambling in Las Vegas. Most Americans, including many who live in cities or states that prohibit gambling, readily accept this arrangement. Zelenskyy has also noted that prostitution is legal in parts of Nevada. He has advocated a similar approach in Ukraine, saying that "society would not mind, as taxes would be paid [by the prostitutes and their workplaces]. Why not give an opportunity to a certain city or territory and [allow prostitution] there?"[25]

Zelenskyy also holds progressive views about the rights of people in the LGBTQ community. During the campaign and after winning the presidency, he had made periodic public remarks signaling his support for equal treatment of all members of society. In 2021, when Zelenskyy met with US president Joe Biden, the two leaders issued a joint statement in which each promised to help the other support human rights. Afterward, Zelenskyy's official presidential website noted his support for the LGBTQ population—and others—that have faced historic discrimination. The presidential site stated:

> With U.S. support, Ukraine will continue to advance respect for human rights, civil liberties, and fundamental freedoms in accordance with international standards and obligations, as well as to fight racism, xenophobia, anti-Semitism, and discrimination against the LGBTQI+ community. Ukraine plans to strengthen accountability for violence against all persons regardless of gender, race, ethnicity, religion, sexual orientation, or political views.[26]

His Biggest Single Issue

The bills regarding the oligarchs and national referenda, along with support for various social issues, were only some of the many topics that kept Zelenskyy busy during his first couple of years in office. The president and his military generals also kept a close eye on the activities of pro-Russian separatists in the Donbas.

In addition, in September 2019 Zelenskyy was forced to devote time and effort to some disturbing requests that US president Donald Trump had made back in late July. In a telephone call, Trump had demanded that his Ukrainian counterpart dig up scandalous dirt about Hunter Biden, son of Trump's opponent in the upcoming 2020 US presidential election—Joe Biden. Be-

Zelenskyy, left, is pictured in the Oval Office of the White House, meeting with US president Joe Biden in 2021. The two leaders issued a joint statement in which each promised to help the other support human rights.

fitting the importance of the caller's office, Zelenskyy politely had fielded the call but had largely ignored Trump's request. In September, feeling pressured by the media to reveal what he and Trump had discussed, the Ukrainian president addressed the issue in two separate press briefings. In both cases he indicated that he had no intention of getting directly involved in what he felt was strictly an internal US matter.

No single issue, however, came even close to preoccupying Zelenskyy's time and attention as president as much as his handling of the Ukrainian response to the global COVID-19 pandemic. Experts on the issue generally agree that his response to the pandemic was strong. In large part, they say, this is because he acted both early in the crisis and much more quickly than most other national leaders. Indeed, the extent of the dangers of the virus was not widely known until mid- to late February 2020, and a majority of nations did not begin to take serious countermeasures until April, May, or even later. In contrast, Zelenskyy reacted swiftly. On March 12, says Emily

Channell-Justice of the Harvard Ukrainian Research Institute, he issued a decree that closed schools for a minimum of three weeks. Channell-Justice writes:

> Transportation, including airlines, interregional trains, and city metros were shut down on March 17. At the same time, restaurants, bars, gyms, and shopping centers were also closed. Only outlets that sold food products, fuel, hygiene products, medicine, and other medical products were allowed to stay open. . . . Throughout March, the government imposed further distancing measures, including a ban on the use of playgrounds and outdoor sports equipment.[27]

A large majority of Ukrainians felt that these early antivirus measures enacted by the Zelenskyy government were prudent and approved of them in interviews and polls. One poll taken in April 2020 indicated that fully 80 percent of the population agreed that banning large-scale public events was necessary. Moreover, over 70 percent of those polled felt the president had no other choice but to temporarily limit the use of cars, trollies, and subways in several of the country's biggest cities. A mere 6 percent of citizens polled felt that Zelenskyy had overreacted to the pandemic.

High Marks for Early Leadership

As happened in other countries worldwide, millions of Ukrainians contracted COVID-19. The period between mid-2020 and mid-2021—before the availability of vaccines—was especially difficult, but smaller numbers of people continued to be affected well into 2022. By June 2022, out of the country's total population of more than 60 million, just over 5,040,000 people had contracted the disease, and almost 112,500 had died from it.

As devastating as these figures seemed to the Ukrainians themselves, the reality was that their nation had come through the pandemic with one of the lowest casualty rates in the world. Only one in twelve Ukrainians had contracted the virus, and just under 0.2 percent of the population had died of it. (In the United States, by comparison, more than one in four people contracted COVID-19, and more than 0.3 percent died of it.)

As a result, Zelenskyy emerged—both inside Ukraine and on the national stage—as a cautious, sensible, caring leader who had handled the crisis as well as anyone could be expected to do. His high marks overall stemmed not only from the country's relatively low casualty figures but also from the way his government dealt with the pandemic's economic impact. Early in the crisis financial experts among Zelenskyy's advisers warned him that as many as half a million or more Ukrainians might lose their jobs because of the widespread shutdowns of businesses, transportation industries, and so forth. And the result

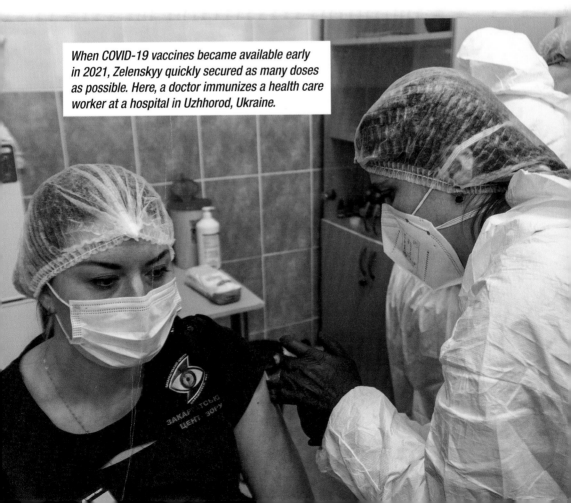

When COVID-19 vaccines became available early in 2021, Zelenskyy quickly secured as many doses as possible. Here, a doctor immunizes a health care worker at a hospital in Uzhhorod, Ukraine.

would likely be widespread poverty and, if the pandemic lasted long enough, possibly even an economic depression. Hoping to avoid such a bleak scenario, the Zelenskyy government distributed unemployment checks to large numbers of citizens. During 2020 and 2021 the Ukrainian government issued an extra $85 million in unemployment payments to its citizens.

Meanwhile, Zelenskyy ordered his nation's health officials to spearhead efforts to battle COVID-19 on the medical front. Money was allotted to buy respirators from various countries to combat a shortage of those lifesaving devices in many Ukrainian hospitals. Also, when the vaccines engineered in the United States became available in early 2021, Zelenskyy secured as many doses as possible. Ukrainian health officials then created more than eight hundred mobile vaccination teams that fanned out across the country in late February 2021. By January 2022, 45 percent of Ukrainians had been vaccinated and boosted. Zelenskyy's high marks for his handling of the pandemic were in general reflective of his overall performance as president in his first three years in office. Although he had critics both inside and outside of Ukraine, their voices were largely drowned out by his

Dealing with a Bigoted Heckler

An incident that took place in 2019 (and was replayed many times on television news programs) reminded Ukrainians of Zelenskyy's views on human rights, including the rights of Ukraine's LGBTQ community. Late that year, Zelenskyy was giving a speech when he was suddenly interrupted. A man wearing a crucifix around his neck yelled in part, "Why haven't you given answers to bishops and all of us that you'll stop the . . . spreading [of the] perversity of homosexuality? [Also] will you prevent the legalization of prostitution and abortions?"

Patiently and in a calm voice, Zelenskyy told the heckler, "Legalization of anything in the country can only be implemented through Ukrainian law." He added, "This means by the hands of the Ukrainian parliament and by approval of laws. Regarding LGBT: I don't want to say anything negative because we all live in an open society where each one can choose the language they speak, their ethnicity, and [sexual] orientation. Leave those [frequently and unfairly persecuted] people finally at peace, for God's sake!"

Quoted in Emma P. Maurice, "Ukraine President Volodymyr Zelensky Shuts Down Homophobic Heckler During Press Conference," PinkNews, October 14, 2019. www.pinknews.co.uk.

supporters and admirers. A number of expert commentators have noted that this former actor and comedian has been generally effective in a difficult, nerve-wracking job. Evaluating the early years of Zelenskyy's presidency, in 2021 college professor Mikhail Minakov, one of the world's leading experts on Ukraine, stated, "Two years after entering the stormy waters of Ukrainian politics, Volodymyr Zelensky is a politically engaged leader who has managed to mobilize support from the citizenry despite unmet expectations. . . . Unlike many presidents before him, Volodymyr Zelensky enjoys an astonishingly high level of trust nationwide."[28]

Chapter Four

Wartime Leader

Nothing during the first three years of Zelenskyy's presidency—not wrestling with corruption, not the COVID-19 pandemic—could have prepared Ukraine's young president for what was to come in 2022. In late 2021 Russian president Vladimir Putin had begun steadily amassing his country's military forces along Ukraine's northern border—a border shared with Russia and its ally Belarus. Putin had also increased Russian naval presence in the Black Sea, an important trade and transportation route for both Russia and Ukraine. US intelligence services warned President Joe Biden, who in turn warned Zelenskyy, that Putin was preparing to launch a major invasion of Ukraine. Pictures of the Russian forces taken by US satellites showed the exact array of weapons and troop transports that would be needed for large-scale combat.

Zelenskyy was less certain that Putin would go that far. The Russians had amassed troops on Ukraine's northern border before, but there had been no full-scale invasion. Referring to the widely publicized US satellite photos, Zelenskyy told reporters at a news conference, "I can see the 100,000 [Russian] soldiers."[29] He went on to note that Putin was probably trying to scare Ukraine's leaders and people.

A reporter asked Zelenskyy why Putin would want to frighten the Ukrainians in such an aggressive manner. Zelenskyy replied that such warlike posturing was likely designed to make the Ukrainians think twice about seeking membership in the European Union (EU) or NATO—moves that Putin vehemently opposed. After the news conference, the Ukrainian president said he was hopeful that Putin was bluffing with the intent of intimidating both the Ukrainians and the Western NATO nations. Moreover, the BBC reported that Zelenskyy told Biden and other Western leaders that their repeated warnings about an imminent invasion might prove counterproductive. They might make large numbers of Ukrainians feel panicky.

The Invasion Begins

As the world now knows, Putin was not bluffing. Early on the morning of February 24, 2022, the Russians began firing missiles into Kyiv and other Ukrainian cities. At the same time, hundreds of tanks and other armored vehicles crossed Ukraine's northern border and headed southward. It was clear that the invaders' aim was to make a lightning strike on Kyiv, seize the city, and topple Zelenskyy's government.

Mere minutes after the invasion commenced, Ukrainian intelligence officers arrived at the presidential residence in Kyiv. They informed Zelenskyy of what was happening, although he had already deduced as much, having been awakened by the sounds of explosions in the distance. After dispensing some preliminary orders to his top aides, he and his wife, Olena, went to their children's rooms, woke them, and told them that their country was at war. Assuming that Putin would come after him and his family, Zelenskyy helped his family prepare to leave their home immediately.

Minutes after the family's departure, a military adviser told the president that parachutes had been spotted descending from the sky in the city's northern sector. It was clear, he advised Zelenskyy, that Putin had dispatched teams of commandos to find and kill Zelenskyy and his family, with the aim of leaving Ukraine leaderless. Indeed, in the hours that followed, some of those assassins actually came close to achieving that goal. At one point a commando team came within only a few hundred yards of Zelenskyy and his chief military advisers. Smart thinking and maneuvering

by the Ukrainian leaders averted a worst-case scenario, however. Zelenskyy, with his family and advisers in tow, initially stayed constantly on the move. The group flitted from one safe house to another in the capital, thereby preventing the assassins from finding their main targets.

That evening, after the presidential entourage had settled down in what appeared to be safe quarters in a central part of the city, some Ukrainian military personnel arrived. They distributed bulletproof vests and assault rifles to Zelenskyy and roughly a dozen of his advisers. Later that night, small teams of American and British military officers entered the quarters and approached Zelenskyy. Arrangements had been made, they told him, to evacuate him and his entourage so that he could escape the country and set up a government in exile. It was at that moment that Zelenskyy soberly told them he required ammunition rather than a ride—words that in less than a day would deeply move people around the world.

A Wartime Versus Peacetime Leader

Zelenskyy's decision to stay in Kyiv and organize the country's defense did much more than capture the imagination of foreigners. It also inspired and rallied the Ukrainian people. News reports showed them that their leader had not only refused to flee but also declined the option of staying relatively safe in a specially constructed presidential bunker located just outside Kyiv. That facility was secure, well stocked with provisions, and capable of withstanding a protracted siege. Zelenskyy could have stayed there with his family for the duration of the war, but he flatly rejected the idea. He chose instead to remain downtown in the capital. There, he could periodically walk the streets and record videos in which he spoke directly to the people and reassured them that their government was still intact and functioning.

Zelenskyy's decision to stay relatively in the open in Kyiv, along with his intermittent addresses to his people, made up only part of an overall display of effective leadership that few people, inside or outside of Ukraine, had expected from him. Indeed, whatever

War Crimes

Almost from the beginning of the Russian invasion, Ukraine's president has accused Russia of committing war crimes. According to Ukrainian investigators who are painstakingly gathering evidence of such crimes, Russian soldiers have indiscriminately destroyed homes and civilian areas, murdered civilians, and dumped their bodies in unmarked mass graves.

Appearing via Zoom on the American investigative news program *60 Minutes* in April 2022, Zelenskyy cited some of the evidence Ukrainian investigators had found up to that point. Ukrainian intelligence had intercepted the voice communications of Russian soldiers, he said, "talking with their parents [about] what they stole and who they abducted. There are recordings of [Russian] prisoners of war who admitted to killing people. There are [Russian] pilots in prison who had maps with civilian targets to bomb. There are also investigations being done based on the remains of the dead."

Still, Zelenskyy explained, the Ukrainians were resisting with all their might. They are fighting, he said, "for [their] existence and for survival. That's the combined heroism of everyone—of the people, of the authorities, of the armed forces. We [have become] a single fist."

Quoted in Catherine Garcia, "Zelensky Shares with *60 Minutes* Ukraine's Evidence of Russian War Crimes," *The Week*, April 10, 2022. https://theweek.com.

his qualities, or in some cases lack of them, as a peacetime president, worldwide opinion now judged him differently. The general conclusion was that he had demonstrated the qualities of a highly effective wartime leader. Many military experts in the United States and other Western countries remarked that he seemed to have an innate sense of what to do to mount a credible defense of his nation.

That capacity, along with the ability to rally the support of a majority of Ukrainians, is a potent combination, those experts say. Analyzing Zelenskyy's overall qualities as a wartime leader, college professor Mikhail Minakov, one of the world's leading experts on Ukraine, admits that in peacetime the former comedian exhibited a mix of strengths and weaknesses. When war was thrust upon him, however,

> he came into his own. Zelensky has turned out to be a tough and courageous wartime leader, perfectly meeting the nation's needs for firm leadership. Despite world leaders' numerous urgings, he has refused to leave Ukraine . . . [and] he remained in Kyiv, despite anticipated assassination attempts, and has day after day served as a model of resistance to the personal and national existential threat. In numerous conversations, Ukrainian soldiers, activists, and businessmen have told me that they joined the defense because the president did not flee. Zelensky inspired Ukrainians to unite around him and defend Ukraine.[30]

Furious, Heroic Resistance

Zelenskyy's efforts immediately bore fruit. The columns of tanks and soldiers that had entered northern Ukraine, bent on capturing Kyiv, largely stalled. This happened in part because the Russian soldiers were poorly led and supplied. But the biggest reason for the invaders' early failure was the steadfast, valiant resistance of Ukrainian soldiers and civilians. That Zelenskyy had managed to unite his people and gather Ukraine's best military leaders and analysts around him produced telling results. In the early days and weeks of the war, Ukrainian forces resisted the invaders furiously and heroically. As a result, the Russians failed to execute their initial military goal. It became clear that Putin had expected his forces to cross the northern border, rapidly surround Kyiv, and force what he assumed would be the disorganized and terrified residents to surrender. Russian military generals had apparently assured Putin that the whole operation would be over in a few days.

Thus, Putin had clearly underestimated both Zelenskyy's ability to rally Ukrainian forces and the brave, superb battlefield performance of those forces. Reports from the front lines by journalists from many countries revealed that many of the Russian troops were either poorly trained, unaware of Putin's overall plan, or both. Even the Russian supply lines were ineptly managed, illustrated by the hundreds of Russian tanks and troop carriers that ran out of gas on Ukrainian roads. In one well-publicized incident, a Ukrainian civilian approached a stalled Russian tank and asked

When Russian troops attempted to capture Kyiv in early 2022, they were met with steadfast resistance from Ukrainian soldiers and civilians. This picture shows a Ukrainian ambush of Russian tanks in Kyiv on March 10, 2022.

Comparisons with Winston Churchill

During the opening days of the Russian invasion, Zelenskyy addressed the British Parliament via Zoom. Afterward, many people compared him to the great British prime minister Winston Churchill, who during World War II famously said his compatriots would fight the enemy on the beaches, in the fields, and in the streets and would never surrender. Zelenskyy told Parliament in part:

> We are the country that is saving people despite having to fight one of the biggest armies in the world. We have to fight the helicopters, rockets. . . .
>
> And I would like to remind you [of] the words that the [citizens of the] United Kingdom have already heard, which are important again. We will not give up and we will not lose. We will fight until the end, at sea, in the air. We will continue fighting for our land, whatever the cost. We will fight in the forests, in the fields, on the shores, in the streets. I'd like to add that we will fight on the banks of different rivers and we're looking for your help, for the help of the civilized countries.

Quoted in *The Guardian* (Manchester, UK), "'Thirteen Days of Struggle': Zelenskyy's Speech to UK Parliament—Transcript," March 8, 2022. www.theguardian.com.

its occupants if they needed a tow back to Russia. Incredibly, instead of shooting the questioner, the tank crew laughed at his joke, and the Ukrainian went on his way.

Yet in spite of his initial success as a wartime leader and the effectiveness of his soldiers, Zelenskyy was well aware that bravery and efficient organization were not enough to win and drive the invaders back. In contrast to Russia's superior weapons arsenal, Ukraine had relatively few tanks, only so much ammunition for its guns, and a limited number of weapons that could destroy enemy tanks and other armored vehicles. Therefore, he correctly reasoned, it was imperative that his country receive weapons, ammunition, and other supplies from the NATO nations and other friendly countries. These included Germany, Poland, France, the United Kingdom, and especially the United States, which has large supplies of the most sophisticated war matériel in the world.

Appeals for Military Aid

In order to secure such aid, Zelenskyy fell back on his strong abilities as a public speaker and film producer. From the standpoint of receiving aid from other nations, the most obvious collective group to approach, he knew, was the European Union because it directly borders Ukraine. He appealed separately to each European nation, requesting whatever weapons, ammunition, and other military supplies its government was able to supply. At the same time, he addressed the leaders of those countries collectively in a Zoom call. They gathered on March 1, 2022, at the EU's large meeting hall in Strasbourg, France.

Clad in an olive-green T-shirt and visible to the EU delegates on an enormous TV screen, Zelenskyy now made a fervent, emotional appeal for his nation's admittance to the organization. The Ukrainians were currently in a desperate struggle for their lives and very existence, he said, adding, "We are fighting for our rights, for our freedom, for our lives, and now we are fighting for our survival. Every [town] square today, no matter what it's called, is going to be called Freedom Square, in every city of our country. No one is going to break us. We are strong. We are Ukrainians."[31]

On March 16, 2022, Zelenskyy delivered a speech to the US Congress, via videoconference. He acknowledged the help that had already been received and appealed to the United States to do more.

Raising a fist in the air, Zelenskyy ended the oration dramatically, exclaiming, "Life will win over death. And light will win over darkness. Glory to Ukraine!"[32] At that moment, every person in the hall sprang to his or her feet and gave Zelenskyy a prolonged standing ovation. Less than an hour later, one of the delegates who had listened to the speech recalled that it had been incredibly powerful and moving, so much so that Zelenskyy's translator openly cried.

Equally important to Ukraine for the war effort, however, Zelenskyy realized, was getting military support from the United States. He spoke privately to Biden, who agreed to send military aid as fast as humanly possible. Zelenskyy also appealed directly to Congress on March 16, 2022. In a speech shown over Zoom, he acknowledged weapons and other aid sent to Ukraine before the war. "Ukraine is grateful to the United States for its overwhelming support," he stated, "for everything that your government and your people have done for us, for weapons and ammunition, for training, for finances, [and so forth]." Nevertheless, he added, much more was now needed. With the Russians invading, it had become "the darkest time for our country, for the whole [of] Europe. I call on you to do more . . . until the Russian military machine stops."[33]

After making this appeal, Zelenskyy knew that two crucial questions loomed. First, would the Americans and Ukraine's other allies agree to send more weapons and other vital matériel? Second, would those supplies be enough to save his nation from falling to Russian aggression? "This is a terror that Europe has not seen, has not seen for 80 years," he told the Americans. "And we are asking for . . . an answer to this terror from the whole world."[34]

Chapter Five

Setting an Example for Democracies Everywhere

On April 19, 2022, the fifty-fifth day of Russia's unprovoked war on Ukraine, Volodymyr Zelenskyy took a few moments out of his busy schedule to rest. Although he tended to move from place to place many times each day, at that moment he was in a concrete bunker in a secret presidential compound hidden in downtown Kyiv. There he greeted Simon Shuster, a noted journalist and war correspondent for *Time* magazine.

Shuster immediately observed that Zelenskyy looked different than when the two had met three years before. Clearly, the crushing responsibilities of being a wartime leader and witnessing so much death and destruction had taken a toll on Zelenskyy. Mostly clean-shaven in the past, he had grown a beard. More importantly, he now bore a somewhat haggard expression and did not smile much.

Near-constant worry will do that to a person, Zelenskyy told Shuster during the interview. It had become something of a habit, the Ukrainian president explained, to lie awake at night and wonder whether he had failed to do something important that day. It was pointless to try to fight that feeling when it came, he said.

I look at [my agenda] several times [per day] and sense that something is wrong. It's my conscience bothering me. I've let myself sleep. But now what? Something [tragic and life-altering] is happening right now [in my country]. People see this war on Instagram, on social media. When they get sick of it, they will scroll away. [That's understandable because] it's a lot of blood [and] a lot of emotion."[35]

Carrying the Weight of a Global Hope

Despite his worries about the war and what it has cost his people, Zelenskyy has not wavered in his resolve. He often tells friends and colleagues that the Russians must be stopped, that they have to be driven back into their own country. Doing so will not only save Ukraine, Zelenskyy told Shuster. It will become a symbolic victory for freedom-loving people everywhere.

Zelenskyy talked with Shuster about how he feels the weight of the world's hopes for a Ukrainian victory. He pointed out, "You understand that they [the world's nations] are watching. [I'm] a symbol. [I] need to act the way the head of [a democratic] state must act."[36]

One of the president's aides, Oleksiy Arestovych, agreed fully with that statement. A veteran of Ukraine's military intelligence

Zelenskyy and His Wife Grant a Wartime Interview

In mid-May 2022, Jennifer Hassan, a well-known London-based reporter for the *Washington Post*, managed to land an exclusive TV interview with Olena Zelenska and her husband, Volodymyr Zelenskyy. One of the many questions Hassan asked was how the Russian invasion had affected the Zelenskyy family. As was true of so many other Ukrainian families, Zelenska answered, the presidential family had been uprooted and stressed out. She confessed that she had not seen her husband very much since the Russian incursion began in February. Indeed, she explained, the couple had more often communicated via telephone than in person. "He lives at his job," Ukraine's First Lady said. "We didn't see him at all for two and a half months." In fact, Zelenska added, she was actually grateful for Hassan's interview because it allowed her and Zelenskyy to enjoy some needed personal time together. It was a sort of "date on TV, thank you," Zelenska quipped. Her husband confirmed her observation with a wry smile and a nod.

Jennifer Hassan, "Ukraine's First Lady Details War's Toll on the Zelensky Family," *Washington Post*, May 22, 2022. www.washingtonpost.com.

In April 2022, a journalist observed that Zelenskyy looked haggard as a result of the stresses of war, with a beard and a more serious demeanor. Zelenskyy is pictured here at a press conference on April 23, 2022.

service who had been, like Zelenskyy, an actor in Kyiv for many years, heaped praise on his boss for being the right kind of president. At times, when the two men met privately and were candid with each other, Arestovych told Shuster, Zelenskyy made "the greatest impression as a man of integrity and humanity."[37] Arestovych believed strongly that Zelenskyy was, for whatever reasons one might deduce, the right leader at the right time, not only for Ukraine's survival, but also for the very idea of democracy and its importance in the world.

Many Powerful and Emotional Appeals

Nothing illustrates that view more clearly than Zelenskyy's seemingly tireless attempts to win support from nations and organizations around the world. Zelenskyy knows better than most that Ukraine's future—its very existence—depends on meeting Russia's military might with similar capabilities. Toward that end, he has made one appeal after another to heads of state, elected lawmakers, and representatives of influential organizations worldwide. Most of his appeals for help have been broadcast over Zoom or other online platforms. Aside from speeches made this way to US and UK lawmakers, he has spoken to leaders in Germany, Italy, Sweden, and Finland in Europe; Jordan and Israel in the Middle East; Kenya and Tunisia in Africa; South Korea and Japan in Asia; and Australia and New Zealand in the Pacific region. In these speeches, most of which he composed himself, Zelenskyy has requested tanks, anti-tank and anti-missile systems, automatic rifles, bulletproof vests and other armor, communications devices of various kinds, and food, medical supplies, and trucks to distribute them.

Zelenskyy has also met personally in Kyiv with various world leaders and other high-ranking foreign officials. Among those who have made the wartime trip to show their support for Zelenskyy and Ukraine are French president Emmanuel Macron, German chancellor Olaf Scholz, Italian prime minister Mario Draghi, British prime minister Boris Johnson, US First Lady Jill Biden, and US secretary of state Antony Blinken. Typical of the benefits of such visits for Zelenskyy and his government were Scholz's public comments made during his Kyiv visit. "We came to Kyiv today with a clear message," he stated. "Ukraine belongs to the European family. Germany wants a positive decision in favor of Ukraine as a European Union candidate country."[38]

A few months later, European leaders followed through on Ukraine's request and the positive comments from Germany and other EU members. On June 23, the European Council (made up of diplomats who map out EU political goals and direction) announced that the organization planned to move forward on

Ukraine's request for full membership. In doing so, the council repeated what it had said several times in prior months—that it stands strongly with Ukraine and that all EU members would provide the Ukrainians with economic, military, and humanitarian aid. Furthermore, the member states firmly condemned Russia's invasion and said they would help Ukraine rebuild its badly damaged infrastructure at the war's conclusion. The council also pledged to hold Russia responsible and accountable for war crimes committed by its soldiers.

Seeking an End to the War

Despite Zelenskyy's anger at Putin's catastrophic and unprovoked invasion of his nation—and the war crimes being committed against his people—the Ukrainian leader has stated several times his desire to meet and negotiate with his Russian counterpart. Zelenskyy emphasized that he would meet *only* with Putin and *not* with any of the Russian president's deputies or other underlings. Zelenskyy stated his belief that a diplomatic solution to the war was possible. The first step in reaching a peace deal, he added, would be for Putin to withdraw his forces to the positions they held before Russia's February invasion of Ukraine. As of early July, Putin had not responded to Zelenskyy's peace overtures.

Meanwhile, Zelenskyy continued his well-publicized efforts to win global support for his country. In April he made virtual appearances at the World Bank, a global financial institution that makes loans to world governments, and at the annual Grammy Awards ceremony. His appeal to the World Bank was intended to garner financial support to back Ukraine's struggle for freedom. In contrast, Zelenskyy's speech to the attendees at the Grammy Awards ceremony and other such entertainment venues was designed to spread the word of Ukraine's plight among ordinary people in the United States and other countries. People everywhere and from all walks of life enjoy music, he pointed out in his speech at the Grammy Awards ceremony. He continued with this powerful message:

"Our musicians wear body armor instead of tuxedos."[39]

—Volodymyr Zelenskyy to the audience of the Grammy Awards ceremony

War. What is more opposite to music? The silence of ruined cities and killed people. Our children draw swooping rockets, not shooting stars. . . . The war doesn't let us choose who survives and who stays in eternal silence. Our musicians wear body armor instead of tuxedos. They sing to the wounded in hospitals, even to those who can't hear them. But the music will break through anyway. We defend our freedom to live, to love, to [make music] on our land. We are fighting Russia, which brings horrible silence with its bombs. The dead silence. Fill the silence with your music. Fill it today to tell our story. Tell the truth about the war on your social networks, on TV. Support us in any way you can. Any [way at all], but not silence. And then peace will come.[39]

Why Ukraine Has the Psychological Advantage

In March 2022, CNN correspondent Matthew Chance interviewed Volodymyr Zelenskyy in Kyiv and asked, among other things, what chances the Ukrainians had against the large numbers of Russian invaders. Zelenskyy's answer emphasized what military experts would call the psychological advantage. This is the idea that the Ukrainians had the advantage because they were fighting for their homes and freedom, whereas most of the Russian soldiers did not even know why they had been sent to fight. That fact, Zelenskyy told Chance,

> should be sent far and wide . . . so [the peoples of the world] will understand what it is like for us here . . . and why support for Ukraine matters. . . . Why are we winning? Why are we defending ourselves? Because this is our home. . . . We have what we need to protect [ourselves]. And [the Russian soldiers] do not even understand our state. They do not know these streets. They do not know our people, do not understand our philosophy, our aspirations, [or] what type of people we are. They do not know anything here. They were just sent here to fight and to die.

Quoted in Matthew Chance, "'This War Is for All the World': Zelensky Says War Is Over Democracy and Freedom," CNN, March 2, 2022. www.cnn.com.

Reckless but Courageous Forays into the Field

Zelenskyy's appeals for foreign aid have occupied only part of his time. He has also spent significant chunks of time and energy on intelligence briefings, analyses of damages and casualties, strategy sessions to decide the best ways to strike back at the enemy, and efforts to protect Ukrainian cities, villages, farms, railways, and so forth.

As happens in most wars, much of the information that has reached Zelenskyy and his top aides has come from operatives in the field. But in his years as president, Zelenskyy has time and again defied tradition and general wisdom. And wartime information gathering has been no exception. As Shuster pointed out, early on in the fighting the Ukrainian president

> insisted on going to see the action for himself. In early March, when the Russians were still shelling Kyiv and trying to encircle the capital, [Zelenskyy] drove out of his compound in secret, accompanied by two of his friends

and a small team of bodyguards. . . . There were no cameras with them. . . . Heading north from Bankova Street, the group went to a collapsed bridge that marked the front line at the edge of the city. It was the first time Zelensky had seen the effects of the fighting up close.[40]

A couple of weeks later, Zelenskyy made another foray outside the safety of his compound. This time he took camera crews with him. Protected by a few armored vehicles and bodyguards, the president inspected the remains of the town of Bucha, where Russian soldiers had gone on a rampage and slaughtered hundreds of unarmed civilians. Zelenskyy said that he personally "found [dead citizens] in barrels, basements, strangled, tortured."[41] These first-hand experiences on the front lines, Zelenskyy told some friends, burned the images of the war's horrors into his mind's eye and made him all the more eager to drive the invaders from his country. "Evil has returned," he stated in a speech to his countrymen,

During the war, Zelenskyy has made numerous risky forays into the active battlefield. He is pictured here on April 4, 2022, visiting the town of Bucha, where Russian soldiers had slaughtered and executed hundreds of unarmed civilians.

comparing Russia's invasion to Nazi Germany's attack on Ukraine some eighty years before. "Decades after World War II, darkness has returned to Ukraine. . . . Evil has returned, in a different uniform, under different slogans, but for the same purpose,"[42] he added—for conquest, subjugation, and oppression.

Zelenskyy's repeated displays of bravery and tenacity and his unflagging determination to defend his nation against a tyrannical adversary have won many admirers. Accordingly, on April 21, 2022, he was one of five individuals chosen to receive the John F. Kennedy Profile in Courage Award. Given annually, that prestigious prize is named after Kennedy's 1957 Pulitzer Prize–winning book, *Profiles in Courage*. The John F. Kennedy Library Foundation, which chooses the recipients, describes the award as honoring people who "have placed their careers and lives on the line to protect democratic principles." Faced with constant danger, the foundation stated, "Zelenskyy has led a courageous defense of democratic ideals and political independence. With candor and clarity, he has focused the eyes of the world on the existential threat facing Ukraine, and on the need for robust, uncompromising international engagement and cooperation to safeguard all democratic societies. His principled leadership has strengthened the resolve of Ukrainians and people around the globe to protect and defend the fragile human right of self-determination."[43]

No Regrets

Considering the dangerous state of affairs in which Ukraine found itself in 2022, some people—both inside and outside of Ukraine—wondered if Zelenskyy regretted having run for and won the presidency. Shuster was one of the foreigners who was curious about how the

> "Evil has returned, in a different uniform, under different slogans, but for the same purpose."[42]
>
> —Volodymyr Zelenskyy

> "Zelenskyy has led a courageous defense of democratic ideals and political independence. . . . His principled leadership has strengthened the resolve of Ukrainians and people around the globe to protect and defend the fragile human right of self-determination."[43]
>
> —John F. Kennedy Profile in Courage Award

Ukrainian leader felt about this. He broached that subject when he interviewed Zelenskyy in April 2022. Shuster asked whether he now regretted that fateful decision. "Not for a second,"[44] Zelenskyy answered. He could not say when the war would end. Nor could he imagine how history would describe and judge him. In that moment, Shuster wrote, Volodymyr Zelenskyy—actor, politician, and patriot—knew only that to go on existing, Ukraine badly needed a wartime president. And like all the other roles he had played in his life, it was one he was ready to take on with every ounce of skill and devotion he possessed.

Source Notes

Introduction: Commitment, Courage, and an Indomitable Spirit

1. Quoted in VOA News, "World Reacts to Russia's Invasion of Ukraine," February 24, 2022. www.voanews.com.
2. Quoted in Sharon Braithwaite, "Zelensky Refuses US Offer to Evacuate, Saying 'I Need Ammunition, Not a Ride,'" CNN, February 26, 2022. www.cnn.com.

Chapter One: From Hometown Boy to Popular Comedian

3. Quoted in Yvette Alt Miller, "Ukraine's President Volodymyr Zelensky: Six Facts," Aish, March 1, 2022. https://aish.com.
4. Quoted in Miller, "Ukraine's President Volodymyr Zelensky."
5. Eric Deggans, "In 'Servant of the People,' Viewers Got a Glimpse of the Future President Zelensky," NPR, March 21, 2022. www.npr.org.
6. Quoted in Deggans, "In 'Servant of the People,' Viewers Got a Glimpse of the Future President Zelensky."
7. Quoted in Deggans, "In 'Servant of the People,' Viewers Got a Glimpse of the Future President Zelensky."

Chapter Two: A Very Modern-Style Politician and Leader

8. Quoted in *Ukrainian Weekly* (Jersey City, NJ), "Volodymyr Zelensky's Inaugural Address," May 24, 2019. www.ukrweekly.com.
9. Quoted in *Ukrainian Weekly* (Jersey City, NJ), "Volodymyr Zelensky's Inaugural Address."
10. Tanya Tanyarattinan and Josh Wilson, "Volodymyr Zelensky: Comedy and Politics," Geohistory, July 22, 2019. https://geohistory.today.
11. Quoted in *Ukrainian Weekly* (Jersey City, NJ), "Volodymyr Zelensky's Inaugural Address."
12. Quoted in *The Guardian* (Manchester, UK), "'Thirteen Days of Struggle': Zelensky's Speech to UK Parliament—Transcript," March 8, 2022. www.theguardian.com.
13. Quoted in *Ukrainian Weekly* (Jersey City, NJ), "Volodymyr Zelensky's Inaugural Address."
14. Quoted in *Ukrainian Weekly* (Jersey City, NJ), "Volodymyr Zelensky's Inaugural Address."
15. Quoted in Leon Aron, "What's Behind Putin's Dirty, Violent Speeches?," February 27, 2022. www.theatlantic.com.
16. Quoted in Tanyarattinan and Wilson, "Volodymyr Zelensky."
17. Quoted in Allen Johnson, "Netflix's 'Servant of the People' Showed Ukrainian President Zelenskyy's Courage Long Before Russia Conflict," Datebook, April 8, 2022. https://datebook.sfchronicle.com.
18. Quoted in *Ukrainian Weekly* (Jersey City, NJ), "Volodymyr Zelensky's Inaugural Address."

Chapter Three: First Three Years as President

19. Quoted in Jonah Fisher, "Zelensky v Oligarchs: Ukraine President Targets Super-Rich," BBC, May 21, 2021. www.bbc.com.

20. Fisher, "Zelensky v Oligarchs."
21. Quoted in Fisher, "Zelensky v Oligarchs."
22. Quoted in Fisher, "Zelensky v Oligarchs."
23. Quoted in Akulenko Olena, "Zelensky Enacts Law on Referendum in Ukraine," UNIAN, April 9, 2021. www.unian.info.
24. Quoted in Olena, "Zelensky Enacts Law on Referendum in Ukraine."
25. Quoted in UNIAN, "Zelensky Supports Legalization of Prostitution, Marijuana in Ukraine: Ukraine Could Have Own Las Vegas," UNIAN, April 18, 2019. www.unian.info.
26. Official Website of the President of Ukraine, "Joint Statement on the U.S.-Ukraine Strategic Partnership," September 1, 2021. www.president.gov.ua.
27. Emily Channell-Justice, "COVID-19 in Ukraine: Assessing the Government's Response," Ukrainian Research Institute, Harvard University, 2022. https://huri.harvard.edu.
28. Mikhail Minakov, "Zelensky's Presidency at the Two-Year Mark," Wilson Center, June 3, 2021. www.wilsoncenter.org.

Chapter Four: Wartime Leader

29. Quoted in BBC News, "Ukraine Crisis: Don't Create Panic, Zelensky Tells West," January 28, 2022. www.bbc.com.
30. Mikhail Minakov, "Zelensky Versus Putin: The Personality Factor in Russia's War on Ukraine," Wilson Center, April 13, 2022. www.wilsoncenter.org.
31. Quoted in Media Entertainment Arts Worldwide, "Full Text of Zelenskyy's Heroic Speech to EU That Brought Members to Their Feet with Emotion," March 1, 2022. https://meaww.com.
32. Quoted in Media Entertainment Arts Worldwide, "Full Text of Zelenskyy's Heroic Speech to EU That Brought Members to Their Feet with Emotion."
33. Quoted in AP News, "Text of Ukraine President Zelenskyy's Address to Congress," March 16, 2022. https://apnews.com.
34. Quoted in AP News, "Text of Ukraine President Zelenskyy's Address to Congress."

Chapter Five: Setting an Example for Democracies Everywhere

35. Quoted in Simon Shuster, "Inside Zelensky's World," *Time*, April 28, 2022. https://time.com.
36. Quoted in Shuster, "Inside Zelensky's World."
37. Quoted in Shuster, "Inside Zelensky's World."
38. Quoted in Sonya Mansoor, "Here's All the World Leaders Who Have Visited Ukraine," *Time*, June 16, 2022. https://time.com.
39. Quoted in Dani Blum and Julia Jacobs, "Volodymyr Zelensky Speaks to Grammys Audience in a Prerecorded Video," *New York Times*, April 3, 2022. www.nytimes.com.
40. Shuster, "Inside Zelensky's World."
41. Quoted in Shuster, "Inside Zelensky's World."
42. Quoted in Agence France-Presse, "Evil Has Returned to Ukraine: Zelensky on World War II Anniversary," NDTV, May 8, 2022. www.ndtv.com.
43. "2022 Profile in Courage Award," John F. Kennedy Presidential Library and Museum, April 21, 2022. www.jfklibrary.org.
44. Quoted in Shuster, "Inside Zelensky's World."

Important Events in the Life of Volodymyr Zelenskyy

1978   On January 25 Volodymyr Zelenskyy is born in the Ukrainian town of Kryvyy Rih.

1995   While in college, forms Kvartal 95, a troupe of comic performers.

1997   Enters Kvartal 95 into an annual TV competition held by the "Club of the Funny and Inventive People."

2003   Marries his high school sweetheart, Olena Kiyashko.

2004   Daughter Oleksandra is born.

2006   Enters and wins the dance contest on the popular TV program *Strictly Come Dancing*.

2012   Stars as Napoléon Bonaparte in the feature film *Rzhevskiy Versus Napoleon*.

2013   Son Kyrylo is born.

2015   Stars in the film *8 New Dates* and begins work on his widely popular TV show, *Servant of the People*.

2018   Produces and codirects the feature film *Me. You. He. She.*

2019   Runs for the presidency of Ukraine and wins.

2021   On November 8 signs a landmark law that safeguards the independence of the National Anti-Corruption Bureau of Ukraine, the key agency in the country's struggle against high-level corruption.

2022   On February 24 declares martial law after Russia invades Ukraine.

On March 1 addresses the European Parliament and asks for the help of the member states.

On March 8 addresses the British Parliament and requests military aid and moral support.

On March 16 speaks to members of the US Congress and emphasizes Ukraine's need for military aid.

On April 5, in a speech to the United Nations, accuses Russia of committing atrocities and criticizes inaction by the world body.

On July 4 Zelenskyy urges the international community to support a $750 billion plan to rebuild Ukraine.

For Further Research

Books

Don Croonenberg, *Zelensky: Clown Versus Tsar*. Deil, Netherlands: Willems Uit-gevers, 2022.

Michael Frizell and Pablo Martinena, *Political Power: Volodymyr Zelensky*. Portland, OR: Tidalwave, 2022.

Andrew L. Urban and Chris McLeod, *Zelensky: The Unlikely Hero Who Defied Putin and United the World*. Washington, DC: Regnery, 2022.

Mary Wood, *Everything Is Possible*. New York: Skyhorse, 2022.

Internet Sources

Arab News, "Zelensky: Only 'Diplomacy' Can End Ukraine War," May 21, 2022. www.arabnews.com.

BBC, "War in Ukraine: Zelensky WW2 Speech Accuses Russia of Nazi Atrocities," May 8, 2022. www.bbc.com.

Emily Burack, "Who Is Ukrainian First Lady Olena Zelenska?," *Town & Country*, May 9, 2022. www.townandcountrymag.com.

Beth Daley, "Volodymyr Zelensky's Appeal Lies in His Service to Ukrainians Above All Else," The Conversation, March 2, 2022. https://theconversation.com.

Yekaterina Filatova, "Zelensky and Biden Agree to Step Up the Fight for LGBT Rights in Ukraine," Union of Orthodox Journalists, September 2, 2021. https://spzh.news.

Jonah Fisher, "Zelensky v Oligarchs: Ukraine President Targets Super-Rich," BBC, May 21, 2021. www.bbc.com.

Jeremy Herb, "Exclusive: Zelensky Says Ukraine Won't Give Up Territory in the East to End War with Russia," CNN, April 17, 2022. www.cnn.com.

James Hookway, "Who Is Volodymyr Zelensky?," *Wall Street Journal*, May 12, 2022. www.wsj.com.

Andrew E. Kramer, "How Zelensky Ended Political Discord and Put Ukraine on a War Footing," *New York Times*, April 25, 2022. www.nytimes.com.

Alina Selyukh et al., "The Ripple Effects of Russia's War in Ukraine Are Changing the World," NPR, May 10, 2022. www.npr.org.

Colleen Walsh, "Putin's Iron Fist vs. Zelensky's Moral Clarity," Harvard Gazette, March 7, 2022. https://news.harvard.edu.

Websites
CIA World Factbook
www.cia.gov/the-world-factbook
This website, which is intended for public use, provides detailed demographic, historic, and cultural information about the countries of the world. Information about Ukraine and Russia can be found by clicking on the "Countries" button at the top of the home page and then using the alphabetical links to the two countries.

Official Website of the President of Ukraine
www.president.gov.ua/en
The official website for the president of Ukraine features a short biography of Volodymyr Zelenskyy and highlights his policies, speeches, and other public statements. It also includes photos and videos of visits with foreign dignitaries.

United with Ukraine, US Department of State
www.state.gov/united-with-ukraine
This portion of the US Department of State website provides information about Ukraine and about US efforts to assist Ukraine during its war with Russia. The site highlights US humanitarian efforts, cybersecurity actions, sanctions imposed on Russia, and more.

Index

Picture Credits

Cover: Ukraine Presidents Office/Alamy Stock Photo

About the Aurthor

Historian and award-winning author Don Nardo has written numerous volumes about wars and warfare throughout the ages, along with biographies of wartime leaders, including Julius Caesar, Abraham Lincoln, Franklin D. Roosevelt, Adolf Hitler, and now Volodymyr Zelenskyy. Nardo, who also composes and arranges orchestral music, lives with his wife, Christine, in Massachusetts.